WEIRD WAYS TO WORK WITH PI

(And have you ever noticed that the spelling of "weird" is weird?)

James Tanton

www.jamestanton.com

© 2012 James Tanton

© 2012 James Tanton

TABLE OF CONTENTS:

WHAT IS PI?	………… 5
A FIRST HINT OF WEIRDNESS: PI FOR A SQUARE	………… 9
THE CIRCUMFERENCE OF A CIRCLE … AND ROPES AROUND THE EARTH	………… 11
THE AREA OF A CIRCLE	………… 15
THE RIGHT DEFINITION OF PI FOR REGULAR POLYGON	………… 19
THE WIRE-CUTTING PUZZLE	………… 23
PI FOR NON-REGULAR POLYGONS	………… 29
RESEARCH: GOING FURTHER WITH PI	………… 33
APPENDIX: WHEN IS PI THE SAME FOR ALL CIRCLES?	………… 37
ANSWERS	………… 43

© 2012 James Tanton

WHAT IS PI?

When asked this question most students answer "3.141..." and rattle off some number of digits. Some adults will answer "twenty-two over seven" (I've never had a student say this) and sometimes a student or adult will simply say "pi is a number."

I need to clarify my question:

What is pi, really? It has something to do with circles. What exactly?

Pushing the question this way usually solicits the answer:

Pi is a special number in mathematics. It is the ratio of the circumference C of a circle to its diameter D. The Greek letter π is used for this number.

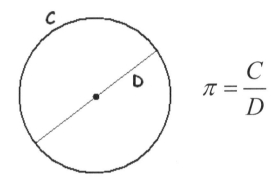

$$\pi = \frac{C}{D}$$

If one takes a piece of string and wraps it along the circumference of a circle, apparently one sees that its length is just over three times the length of the diameter of the circle.

ACTIVITY   Have you ever actually done this? Take a glass and sit it upside down on a sheet of paper. Trace around the rim of the glass so that you have a copy of the circle on the paper. Now wrap a string around the glass. Is the circumference of the circle indeed a tad more than three times the width of the circle?

BETTER YET ... Wrap the string around the glass **seven** times. Compare that length to **twenty-two** times the diameter of the circle!

© 2012 James Tanton

Over the centuries folk have wrapped pieces of string around circles and have noticed they always seem to be the same fraction of units over three times the width of the circle. It appears that the same number comes up over and over again as the ratio of the circumference of a circle to its diameter:

$$\pi = 3.14159265...$$

COMMENT: Pinning down this number has been a long and difficult challenge for scholars over the centuries. It wasn't until the mid-1700s that mathematicians managed to prove that – annoyingly – the decimal expansion of pi goes on forever, with absolutely no repeating pattern to it.

ANOTHER COMMENT: In past decades it was very popular to use the fraction $\frac{22}{7}$ as a number that closely approximates π. We have:

$$\frac{22}{7} = 3.142857...$$

If you did the activity on the previous page you should have seen that seven circumferences of a circle is very very close to equaling twenty-two diameters!

ONE SERIOUS PROBLEM ...

When measuring circles, their circumferences and diameters, we human beings seem to always choose circles of roughly the same size, namely human-scale size.

Maybe the circles we have checked over the centuries have been too small to truly see if the circumference divided by the diameter is the same number every time. **Has anyone checked the circumference and the diameter of a circle the size of the solar system?**

Or maybe the circles we have checked over the centuries have been too big to truly see if the circumference divided by the diameter is the same every time. **Has anyone checked the circumference and the diameter of a circle the size of an atom?**

> **ACTIVITY** Go to Nevada with a friend. Have your friend stand in the middle of the state at one end of a very long rope and, with you at the other end, swing the rope around to draw a large circle the size of the state. Measure the

> circumference and diameter of the circle you drew and divide the two numbers. Do you get a value very close to 3.14159265…?

Most people have been trained to think:

> "Of course, the ratio of circumference to diameter is the same for all circles, even for ones the size of Nevada."

What makes them say "of course"? I bet they have never actually checked.

So …

> **IMPORTANT QUESTION:**
> Is it all obvious that the value of π is the same for all circles?
>
> Here's a small circle and a large one.
>
>
>
> Is it true that the ratio of the circumference to diameter is the same for each, even to the millionth decimal place?

Most people choose to **believe** that the value of pi is the same for all circles. At the human-scale at which we operate this seems to be true, and this is why people probably choose to believe it. But it would be good to know the reasons as to when we should, or shouldn't, believe this to be so.

In the APPENDIX to this pamphlet we get to the behind-the-scenes geometry of pi that tells us when/if we should believe it the same value of for all circles. The appendix assumes you have taken a basic course in geometry,

For now … Let's follow the crowd and see what happens if we believe in the constancy of pi.

BY THE WAY …
If you do the activity for drawing a circle the size of Nevada you **will not** see the value 3.14159265… appearing as pi for that circle!!!

© 2012 James Tanton

A Little Question: Find an example of a drinking glass that is taller than its circumference. (Find one with non-tapered vertical sides).

height > circumference

Can you find one?

If you don't succeed, because none of the glasses you measure have this property, what do you think such a glass would look like? Would a short squat glass more likely have this property or a tall thin one?

A FIRST HINT OF WEIRDNESS: Pi FOR A SQUARE

Who said that a concept of "pi" applies only for circles?

Consider, for instance, a square. We can still talk about its "circumference" (namely, perimeter) and its "diameter." Unfortunately, the measure of the diameter of a square varies, but we can agree to work with the "short diameter" of the square, for example. Then the ratio perimeter to short diameter is the "short" value of π for a square.

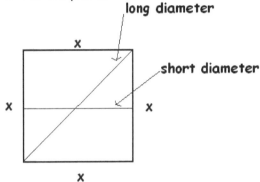

perimeter = 4x

short diameter = x

We get:

$$\pi_{square} = \frac{\text{perimeter}}{\text{short diameter}} = \frac{4x}{x} = 4$$

The (short) value of π for a square is 4. Notice that this value is the same for all squares – big or small.

---

1. EXERCISES:

a) What is the long value of π for a square? Is it the same for all squares?

b) What is the value of π for an equilateral triangle? Use the length of one of the altitudes of the triangle for the diameter.

c) What is the short value of π for a regular hexagon?

PROJECT FOR THOSE WHO KNOW TRIGOMETRY …

d) Compute the values of π for a regular heptagon, octagon, nonagon and decagon (or a regular N-gon). For ease, always use a "diameter" that intersects a side at a right angle.

To what number do these values seem to approach?

The answers appear at the back of this pamphlet.

© 2012 James Tanton

THE CIRCUMFERENCE OF A CIRCLE
... AND ROPES AROUND THE EARTH

We have that $\pi = \dfrac{C}{D}$. It follows then that $C = \pi D$.

Many people prefer to write this formula in terms of the radius r of the circle. Since $D = 2r$ we have:

$$C = 2\pi r$$

ROPE-WRAPPING PUZZLE:
These problems have surprising answers!

a) I have a rope long enough to wrap snugly around the equator of the Earth. I add ten feet to its length. When I wrap the extended rope around the equator it magically hovers just above the ground. How high off the ground is this rope?

b) I do the same thing for the planet Mars, that is, add ten feet of length to a rope that fits snugly about its equator. Again, the extended rope hovers just above the ground. How high off the ground?

c) I do the same thing for the planet the size of a pea, that is, add ten feet of length to a rope that fits snugly about its (tiny) equator. Again, the extended rope hovers just above the ground. How high off the ground?

Really have a go at answering these questions. There is no need to look up any information about radii of planets on the internet. All the details needed are given in the questions!

The answers appear on the next page. (Don't peak until you are ready!). They also appear in the video http://www.jamestanton.com/?p=688.

© 2012 James Tanton

The three puzzles are surprising in three ways:

1. They all have the same answer!

2. They can be computed with no knowledge of the radius of the planet under consideration

and

3. The shared answer is surprisingly large, about 1.6 feet.

Think about this: adding just ten feet to a rope the length of the circumference of the Earth produces enough space to squirm your way under!

Here's one way to approach these problems.

We need to examine two concentric circles with the circumference of one ten feet longer than the other. Call the radius of the inner circle (the equator of the planet) R and let the gap between the two circles be h. (Thus the outer circle, the hovering rope, has radius $R+h$.)

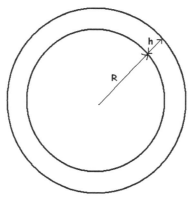

The outer circle has circumference ten feet longer than then inner circle. This means:
$$2\pi(R+h) = 2\pi R + 10$$

Algebra allows us to compute h, without the knowing R:
$$2\pi R + 2\pi h = 2\pi R + 10$$
$$2\pi h = 10$$
$$h = \frac{5}{\pi}$$

That is, $h = \frac{5}{\pi} \approx 1.6 \ feet \approx 19 \ inches$. Wow!!

Weird Ways to Work with Pi

ACTIVITY

These puzzles provide a wonderful activity. Using a length of rope as a fixed radius, draw a circle on the ground with sidewalk chalk. Lay a long rope about its circumference and add ten feet to its length. Have a group of students - evenly spaced about the circle - attempt to wrap this extended rope about the original circle with a gap of constant width. When done, verify that the gap is about 19 inches wide. Repeat this activity with a very small circle drawn on the ground. It is a surprise to see the same gap of 19 inches appear.

There is nothing special about circles in these problems.

2. EXERCISE: *A rope ten feet longer than the perimeter of a square is used to produce a concentric square. Verify that the gap between the two squares is guaranteed to be 1.25 feet.*

3. EXERCISE: *A rope ten feet longer than the perimeter of an equilateral triangle is used to produce a concentric equilateral triangle. Verify that the gap between the triangles is guaranteed to be (to two decimal places) 0.96 feet.*

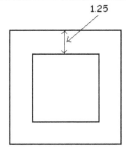 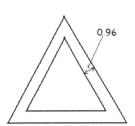

Notice that $1.25 = \dfrac{5}{4}$ and $0.96 \approx \dfrac{5}{3\sqrt{3}}$. The numbers "4" and "$3\sqrt{3}$" have special meaning.

More on this later.

© 2012 James Tanton

4. ASIDE... THE SMOOT

The Harvard Bridge across the Charles River in Boston, Massachusetts connects Cambridge to the Back Bay. Despite its name, it lies directly across from M.I.T.

In 1958, members of the M.I.T. Lambda Chi Alpha fraternity elected their shortest member, Oliver Smoot, to be the unit of measure for measuring the length of the bridge. Fraternity brothers laid Smoot end-to-end across the entire extent of the bridge and found its length to be 364.4 Smoots and one ear. They painted ten Smoot marker points along the bridge and to this day, M.I.T. students repaint those markers each and every year.

It is said by some that Smoot did not actually lie on the ground, but the fraternity constructed a circular wheel with circumference equal to Smoot's height and used the wheel to measure the length of the bridge.

In 1958, Smoot was 170 cm tall. If a wheel was indeed constructed for this task, what was its radius?

Construct a wheel with circumference the height an elected member of your community. Map distances across your school campus using this person's height as the unit of measure!

COMMENT: In 2005, St. Mark's School in Southborough, Massachusetts nominated the Ganz as its official unit of measure!

THE AREA OF A CIRCLE

We have all been taught at an early age that the area A of a circle of radius r is given by the formula:

$$A = \pi r^2$$

I personally find this formula very surprising. Here's why:

The number π is the ratio of the circumference of a circle to its diameter – there is no mention of "area" in its definition. So why should the number π appear in a formula about area? (Do I think too hard?) All we can say from the definition of π is that $\pi = \dfrac{C}{D} = \dfrac{C}{2r}$ (where C is circumference, and D is diameter). This yields the formula $C = 2\pi r$ which is not a statement about area.

How then, do we find the area of a circle?

Here's what most people do ...

Imagine that a given circle is a pizza pie with crust. Divide the circle into eight "pizza wedges" and rearrange them to form a crude (very crude) rectangle:

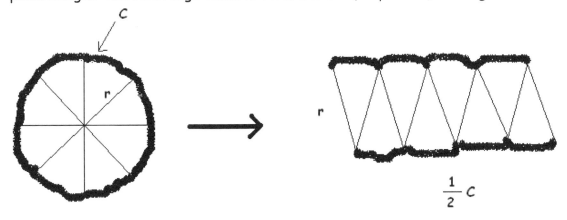

COMMENT: One trouble with writing a book is that one gives away answers too soon. Who would think to arrange pizza slices into a zig-zag design? This is not at all an easy thing to think to do! I apologise for taking away the fun of coming across this joyful epiphany on your own.

© 2012 James Tanton

Notice that half the crust of the pizza lies on the bottom of the crude rectangle and half lies along the top. Thus the length of the "rectangle" is approximately $\frac{1}{2}C$. Notice too that the height of the "rectangle" is approximately r.

This shows that the area of the circle is <u>approximately</u> the area of a rectangle of length $\frac{1}{2}C$ and height r. We have:

$$\text{Area of Circle} \approx \frac{1}{2}C \times r$$

But this is only an approximate formula. Could we do better?

A THOUGHT EXERCISE PROBABLY NOT WORTH ACTUALLY DOING:
Dividing the circle into just eight pizza wedges does not yield a very convincing "rectangle."

a) Draw a large circle on a piece of paper and divide it into 16 pizza wedges. Physically cut them out and arrange them in a "rectangle." What is the approximate length and height of the "rectangle" in terms of C and r? Does the figure reasonably approximate a proper rectangle?

b) Draw another large circle, and this time divide it into at least 32 pizza wedges. Cut them out and rearrange the wedges. Does the resulting figure look more like a true rectangle?

c) Divide a large circle into 100 pizza wedges. Would the approximation to being a rectangle likely be more exact? How about 1000 pizza wedges?

d) Would you be willing to believe that if we could do more and more pizza slices we would get better and better approximations to a true rectangle? Is it reasonable to say that the area of a circle really *is* the area of the ideal rectangle?

COMMENT: There is a "leap of faith" here. We've worked with an approximation and have "taken it to the limit." It is now a matter of intellectual belief to say that the approximation becomes exact in the case of infinitely many infinitely small pizza wedges. (What does that actually mean?)

Most people are willing to accept the "leap of faith" outlined in the previous activity (are you one of those people?) and say that the approximation for the area of the circle of radius r really does become more and more exact, so that the area of the circle truly does equal $A = \frac{1}{2} C \times r$.

One trouble: There is no appearance of the number π here.

Well, it is not actually a trouble. Since our formula involves the number C, which <u>does</u> use the number π, we can substitute $C = 2\pi r$ into the area formula to get:

$$A = \frac{1}{2} C \times r = \frac{1}{2} \times 2\pi r \times r = \pi r^2$$

We have the classic formula after all (via a "leap of faith").

---

5. QUESTION OF HISTORICAL INTEREST:

The oldest known mathematical manuscript, the Rhind papyrus, dated ca 1650 B.C.E. (and believed to be a copy of an even earlier Egyptian text) describes the following approximation for π:

"The area of a circle is approximately the area of a square whose side is one ninth of the circle's diameter less."

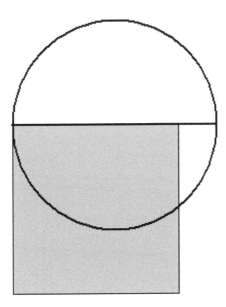

According to this description, what was the ancient Egyptian approximate value for π? Is it better or worse than the approximation $\frac{22}{7}$?

© 2012 James Tanton

THE RIGHT DEFININTION OF PI FOR REGULAR POLYGONS

We have two classic formulas for the circumference and area of the circle:

$$C = 2\pi r$$

$$A = \pi r^2$$

And we have been slightly weird and defined the value of pi for a square to be four.

$$\pi_{square} = 4$$

This was the "short" value of pi found by using the short diameter of a square. Notice that this short diameter is double the short radius (apothem).

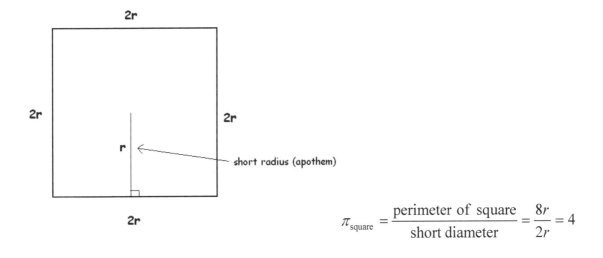

$$\pi_{square} = \frac{\text{perimeter of square}}{\text{short diameter}} = \frac{8r}{2r} = 4$$

And this short value of pi is the right one for a square in the following sense.

> **6. EXERCISE:**
> a) Show that the formula $C = 2\pi r$ works for a square.
> b) Show that the formula $A = \pi r^2$ works for a square.

See also the video: http://www.jamestanton.com/?p=690.

© 2012 James Tanton

Going further ...

For a circle of radius r we have: $\pi_{circle} = \dfrac{C}{2r}$

For a square, we copied this same formula using the short radius (apothem) for r.

Crossing our fingers let's see if this approach is the right one for equilateral triangles too. Set:
$$\pi_{triangle} = \dfrac{\text{perimter of triangle}}{2 \times \text{apothem}}$$

---

7. EXERCISE (SLIGHTLY ANNOYING)
a) Show that $\pi_{triangle} = 3\sqrt{3}$ for all equilateral triangles.
b) Show that the formula $C = 2\pi r$ works for an equilateral triangle.
c) Show that the formula $A = \pi r^2$ works for an equilateral triangle.

This is grand! Boldly continuing on let's define pi for a regular N-gon to be:

$$\pi_{n\text{-gon}} = \dfrac{\text{perimeter}}{2 \times \text{apothem}}$$

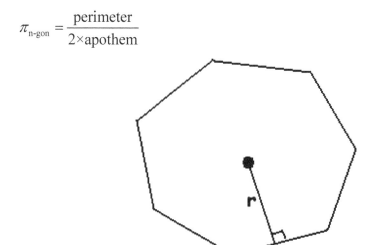

---

8. EXERCISE (VERY ANNOYING!)
a) Show that pi for a regular N-gon is always $N \tan(\dfrac{180}{N})$. (There is a difference from exercise 1 d): we're using a special radius now each time.)
b) Show that the formula $C = 2\pi r$ still works.
c) Show that the formula $A = \pi r^2$ still works.

We shall see on page 29 that there is still a better – and easier- way to think of all this!

© 2012 James Tanton

COMMENT: In the earlier sections we have had long and short (and intermediate) possible values of pi, based on the different types of diameters we could examine. This section shows that thinking in terms of "diameter" is misleading: It is better to think in terms of radius, the short radius in fact, and then all magically holds together!

Note, we can define "diameter" as $2r$, if we like – but it might not correspond to an actual length of a diameter in the polygon. For example, consider an equilateral triangle. If r is a short radius, then $2r$ seems too short be an actual diameter. But the math seems to want us to go with $2r$ nonetheless.

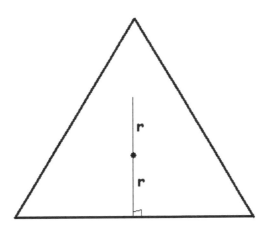

SUMMARY:

For a regular polygon, let r be the length of its short radius (apothem). Define

$$\pi_{polygon} = \frac{perimeter}{2r}$$

Then the formulas $C = 2\pi r$ and $A = \pi r^2$ work for the polygon!

---

9. ROPES FOR ALL REGULAR POLYGONS!

A rope ten feet longer than the perimeter of a regular polygon is wrapped about the polygon to produce a concentric regular polygon. Verify that the gap between the polygons is sure to be $\dfrac{5}{\pi_{polygon}}$ feet.

Everything hangs together! This really is the right definition of pi for a regular polygon.

THE WIRE-CUTTING PUZZLE

Here's another classic problem. Its solution provides more credence to the idea that we have hit upon the right approach to pi.

> A wire of length 1 meter is to be cut into two pieces. The left piece will be bent into a circle and the right piece into a square. The area of each shape shall be computed and the two values added together.
>
> Where along the wire should one make the cut so as to obtain two shapes with the smallest sum of areas? Biggest sum of areas?

This is a tricky problem and you might like to try solving it before reading on. Many calculus books include this problem in their chapters on "max/min problems" but you don't actually need any calculus to solve it.

COMMENT: For a video on this puzzle and all that follows in this section see: http://www.jamestanton.com/?p=1044.

A clever pi-like way to solve this problem appears next.

We know that area of a circle is πr^2 and the area of the square is also "πr^2", and all we have to do to answer this puzzle is add these two areas together and see when that formula is the smallest and largest it can be!

Of course, we have to be careful about which radii and which values of pi we are using for each of the two shapes! Let's sort out some notation.

Call the length of the left piece of wire x so that the right piece has length $1-x$.

Let a be the apothem (radius) of the circle, and b the apothem of the square, and let π_a ($=3.141...$) be the value of pi for circle and $\pi_b(=4)$ its value of a square.

Now the circumference of the circle is:

$$2\pi_a a = x \text{ which gives } a = \frac{x}{2\pi_a}$$

The circumference of the square is:

$$2\pi_b b = 1-x \text{ which gives } b = \frac{1-x}{2\pi_b}$$

The area of the circle is:

$$A_{circle} = \pi_a a^2 = \pi_a \left(\frac{x}{2\pi_a}\right)^2 = \frac{1}{4\pi_a}x^2$$

The area of the square is:

$$A_{square} = \pi_b b^2 = \pi_b \left(\frac{1-x}{2\pi_b}\right)^2 = \frac{1}{4\pi_b}(1-x)^2$$

And the sum of the two areas is:

$$SumAreas = \frac{1}{4\pi_a}x^2 + \frac{1}{4\pi_b}(1-x)^2$$

We need to find which value of x makes this formula the smallest/biggest.

© 2012 James Tanton

Let's expand $(1-x)^2 = 1 - 2x + x^2$ to write:

$$SumAreas = \left(\frac{1}{4\pi_a} + \frac{1}{4\pi_b}\right)x^2 - \frac{1}{2\pi_b}x + \frac{1}{4\pi_b}$$

This is a quadratic in the variable x that takes the value $\frac{1}{4\pi_b} = \frac{1}{16}$ at $x = 0$ and value $\frac{1}{4\pi_a} \approx \frac{1}{12}$ at $x = 1$. We see that the maximum sum of areas occurs for $x = 1$.

We have solved one part of the puzzle: *For the maximum sum of areas ... Don't cut the wire. Use all of it to make a circle!*

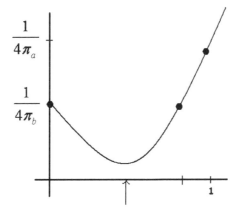

To find the value of x that gives the minimum sum of areas we need to locate the vertex of the quadratic. Most people have memorized the formula $x = -\frac{b}{2a}$ for the location of the vertex. I haven't – so allow me to be a little weird and play with the formal a little more. We have:

$$SumAreas = x\left(\left(\frac{1}{4\pi_a} + \frac{1}{4\pi_b}\right)x - \frac{1}{2\pi_b}\right) + \frac{1}{4\pi_b}$$

Factoring out the x form the first two terms makes it clear that:

Putting $x = 0$ gives $SumAreas = \frac{1}{4\pi_b}$

and

© 2012 James Tanton

Putting $\left(\dfrac{1}{4\pi_a} + \dfrac{1}{4\pi_b}\right)x - \dfrac{1}{2\pi_b} = 0$, that is, $x = \dfrac{\dfrac{1}{2\pi_b}}{\dfrac{1}{4\pi_a} + \dfrac{1}{4\pi_b}}$

also gives $SumAreas = \dfrac{1}{4\pi_b}$

We have two inputs giving symmetrical outputs. The vertex must be halfway between $x = 0$ and this weird value of x.

The value of x that gives the minimum sum of areas is

$$x = \dfrac{1}{2} \times \dfrac{\dfrac{1}{2\pi_b}}{\dfrac{1}{4\pi_a} + \dfrac{1}{4\pi_b}} = \dfrac{\dfrac{1}{4\pi_b}}{\dfrac{1}{4\pi_a} + \dfrac{1}{4\pi_b}}$$

Fractions within fractions are hard to read. Let's multiply the numerator and denominator each by $4\pi_b$.

$$x = \dfrac{1}{\dfrac{\pi_b}{\pi_a} + 1}$$

And again each by π_a:

$$x = \dfrac{\pi_a}{\pi_a + \pi_b}$$

Notice that for this x-value we have $1 - x = \dfrac{\pi_a + \pi_b}{\pi_a + \pi_b} - \dfrac{\pi_a}{\pi_a + \pi_b} = \dfrac{\pi_b}{\pi_a + \pi_b}$

Here is the remarkable way to think about this minimal answer:

The left piece of wire has length $x = \dfrac{\pi_a}{\pi_a + \pi_b}$ *and the right piece* $1 - x = \dfrac{\pi_b}{\pi_a + \pi_b}$. *These lengths come in the ratio* $\dfrac{x}{1-x} = \dfrac{\pi_a}{\pi_b}$.

Weird Ways to Work with Pi

SUMMARY:

To cut a piece of wire so that the areas of a circle (made from the left piece) and a square (made from the right piece) has smallest possible sum, cut the wire at a position that gives the same ratio as the pi-values for those shapes!

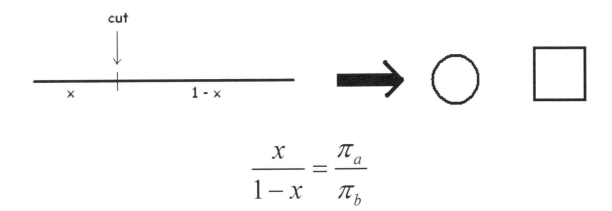

$$\frac{x}{1-x} = \frac{\pi_a}{\pi_b}$$

To add to the fun of it ... Look at the ratio of the areas of those two shapes.

We have seen $A_{circle} = \frac{1}{4\pi_a}x^2$ and $A_{square} = \frac{1}{4\pi_b}(1-x)^2$ and so:

$$\frac{A_{circle}}{A_{square}} = \frac{4\pi_b}{4\pi_a}\left(\frac{x}{1-x}\right)^2 = \frac{4\pi_b}{4\pi_a}\left(\frac{\pi_a}{\pi_b}\right)^2 = \frac{\pi_a}{\pi_b}$$

At the minimal cut the position, the two shapes produced have areas that are also in the ratio of the pi-values for the shapes.

More remarkable still ... We never really used that fact that the shapes produced were a circle and a square. The same result holds for any shapes for which the formulas $C = 2\pi r$ and $A = \pi r^2$ hold.

Always cut the wire at a position so that the two lengths have the same ratio as the pi-values of the shapes under consideration! This produces the smallest sum of areas.

© 2012 James Tanton

COMMENT FOR THOSE WHO KNOW CALCULUS:
As mentioned, one can solve this problem via techniques of calculus. A slick approach is not to think of x as the variable here, but the apothem a instead.

We have the equation $2\pi_a a + 2\pi_b b = 1$ and we wish to minimize $A = \pi_a a^2 + \pi_b b^2$.
To find the location of the minimal area we need to solve $\dfrac{dA}{da} = 0$.
Differentiating the first equation with respect to a gives $\dfrac{db}{da} = -\dfrac{\pi_a}{\pi_b}$ and differentiating the second gives $\dfrac{dA}{da} = 2a\pi_a + 2b\pi_b \dfrac{db}{da}$. Setting this equal to zero and solving quickly yields $a = b$. Thus the two shapes have the same apothem at the optimal position and hence the ratio of their circumferences (and areas for that matter) is $\dfrac{\pi_a}{\pi_b}$.

---

10. A MIGHTY TOUGH CHALLENGE:
A piece of wire is cut into three pieces. The left piece is bent to make a circle, the middle piece an equilateral triangle, and the right piece a regular heptagon. Where should one make the two cuts so as to give a smallest total sum of areas of the three shapes?

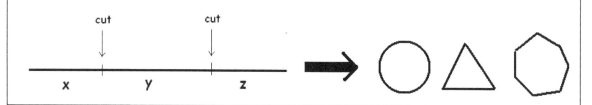

Wouldn't it be remarkable if the solution were to cut sections of lengths in the same ratio as the pi-values of the shapes:

$$x : y : z = \pi_a : \pi_b : \pi_v$$

and wouldn't it be furtherly remarkable if the ratio of the areas of the optimal shapes was also in the same ratio of pi values.

Care to think about this, and the challenge of more cutting and bending wire into more than three shapes?

© 2012 James Tanton

PI FOR NON-REGULAR POLYGONS

Regular polygons are still very nice and still intimately connected with circles: Each regular polygon with short radius r circumscribes a circle of radius r.

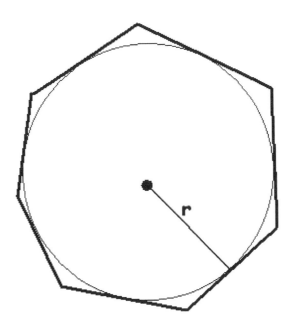

Maybe this explains why working with the short radius was the right thing to do for defining pi for these shapes.

To put this to the test, let's consider any random polygon that circumscribes a circle of radius r and define

$$\pi_{polygon} = \frac{perimeter}{2r}$$

Do the formulas $C = 2\pi r$ and $A = \pi r^2$ work?

NOTE: Clearly the formula $C = 2\pi r$ holds. It follows immediately from how we have chosen to define pi: $perimeter = 2r\pi_{polygon}$. It is the area formula that is the tricky one.

© 2012 James Tanton

Here is a pentagon of side-lengths a, b, c, d, e circumscribing a circle of radius r.

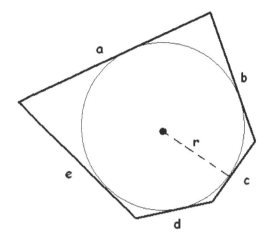

Here the perimeter is $a + b + c + d + e$ and so our definition of pi says:

$$\pi_{polygon} = \frac{a + b + c + d + e}{2r}$$

for this polygon. The question is:

Is this the right definition of pi? Do we have $A = \pi_{polygon} r^2$ for this polygon?

To compute the area of the polygon, divide the polygons into five triangles each of height r.

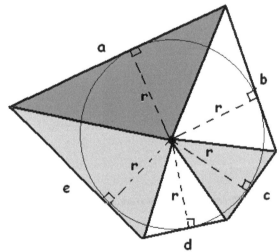

Then we see:

$$\text{Area of Polygon} = \frac{1}{2}ar + \frac{1}{2}br + \frac{1}{2}cr + \frac{1}{2}dr + \frac{1}{2}er = \frac{1}{2}(a+b+c+d+e)r$$

© 2012 James Tanton

But $a+b+c+d+e = perimeter = 2r\pi_{polygon}$. Thus:

$$\text{Area of Polygon} = \frac{1}{2} \times 2r\pi_{polygon} \times r = \pi_{polygon} r^2$$

Fabulous!

It is clear that this same approach works for a polygon of any number of sides circumscribing a circle.

SUMMARY:

For any polygon that circumscribes a circle of radius r, define

$$\pi_{polygon} = \frac{perimeter}{2r}$$

Then the formulas $C = 2\pi_{polygon} r$ and $A = \pi_{polygon} r^2$ hold for that polygon.

(This definition agrees with how we defined pi for regular polygons.)

And coming full circle (!) ...

11. EXERCISE:

a) **ROPE-WRAPPING:** Ten feet of rope is added to the perimeter of a polygon that circumscribes a circle of radius r. This longer rope is used to make a slightly larger scaled copy of the polygon. Prove that it circumscribes a circle of radius $r + \dfrac{5}{\pi_{polygon}}$ feet.

b) **WIRE-CUTTING:** A piece of wire one-meter long is cut. The left piece is bent to make a polygon of one particular shape that circumscribes a circle, and the right piece another polygon of different shape that also circumscribes a circle. Show that, in order to minimize the sum of areas of the two shapes, one should cut the wire so the two pieces have lengths in ratio of the pi-values of the two shapes.

© 2012 James Tanton

12. EXERCISE: Pi for Right Triangles

One proves in a geometry course that every triangle circumscribes a circle. (The center of that "in-circle" is the point where the three angle bisectors of the triangle meet.)

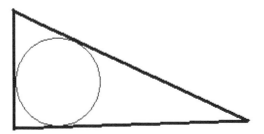

Consider a right triangle with legs of length a and b, and hypotenuse of length c.

a) Show that the radius of the in-circle for this right triangle is given by
$$r = \frac{ab}{a+b+c}.$$

[HINT: Compute the area of the right triangle two different ways.]

b) Use the relation $a^2 + b^2 = c^2$ to show that this can be rewritten
$$r = \frac{1}{2}(a+b-c).$$

c) What is the value of pi for a right triangle?

OPTIONAL: Prove that if a,b,c are integers representing the sides of a right triangle, then $r = \frac{1}{2}(a+b-c)$ is also an integer. Is there an integer right triangle with $r = 1$? $r = 2$? $r = 3$? ...

RESEARCH: GOING FURTHER WITH PI

For polygons, like regular polygons, that circumscribe a circle, there is a natural radius associated with the figure, namely the radius of that in-circle, leading to a natural and good definition of pi:

$$\pi_{polygon} = \frac{perimeter}{2r}$$

The formulas $C = 2\pi r$ and $A = \pi r^2$ then hold.

But not every polygon circumscribes a circle. Further, not every shape is a polygon!

Is it possible to define a meaningful value of pi for any shape?

What is the right value of pi for this shape and all scaled versions of it?

The challenge is to find meaningful values of "r" and "π" for any shape so that the formulas $C = 2\pi r$ and $A = \pi r^2$ hold. (Here C is the perimeter of the shape.)

© 2012 James Tanton

Well... One approach is to think of $C = 2\pi r$ and $A = \pi r^2$ as two formulas in two unknowns, namely, the unknowns of r and π! Let's solve for them:

$$C = 2\pi r \text{ gives } \pi r = \frac{C}{2}$$

$$A = \pi r \times r = \frac{1}{2}Cr \text{ gives } r = \frac{2A}{C}.$$

Substituting back into the first equation yields:

$$\pi = \frac{C}{2r} = \frac{C^2}{4A}$$

SUMMARY:

For any shape of perimeter C and area A, set:

$$r = \frac{2A}{C} \quad \text{and} \quad \pi = \frac{C^2}{4A}$$

Then, by design, the formulas $C = 2\pi r$ and $A = \pi r^2$ hold for that shape.

One shouldn't get excited by this. It is not at all clear from these formula what $r = \frac{2A}{C}$ means, and what $\pi = \frac{C^2}{4A}$ means! Our research challenge, which might or might not pan out to be anything exciting, is to see if these formulas actually have any geometric meaning.

13. EXERCISE: Perimeter is a length and area is a length squared.

a) Show that the formula $r = \frac{2A}{C}$ demonstrates that r, whatever it is, has units of length. (This is good, I suppose.)

b) Show that the formula $\pi = \frac{C^2}{4A}$ demonstrates that π has no units – it is just a number. (Also good?)

14. EXERCISE: Consider a polygon that circumscribes a circle. Show that $\dfrac{2A}{C}$ really does equal the radius of the incircle.

This shows that defining $r = \dfrac{2A}{C}$ does indeed have the right geometric meaning in the context of all the polygons we have discussed thus far.

Now comes the research challenge …

1. Consider a rectangle with one side a units long and the other b units long.

What is the value of $r = \dfrac{2A}{C}$ for such a rectangle? If we draw a circle of this radius with center of the center of the rectangle, does this circle have any obvious geometric properties? (Compare light and dark shaded areas in the picture below!) Would one naturally think of this circle if we didn't first have the formula $r = \dfrac{2A}{C}$?

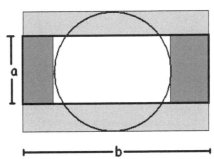

COMMENT: This final question represents the crux of the research matter. For each regular polygon there is a natural circle that comes to mind first – the incircle – which then allows us to create a natural definition of pi for the polygon. For rectangles, it would be nice to consider a "natural" circle for it first, to then define a pi-value for the shape. The formula $r = \dfrac{2A}{C}$ is devoid of any natural geometric context.

2. Repeat this work for other classes of shapes. Develop a general geometric meaning for a circle of radius $\dfrac{2A}{C}$ located at some "center" for a shape!

HAVE FUN!

© 2012 James Tanton

ONE MORE QUERY …

The surface area SA and the volume V and of a sphere of radius r are given by the formulas:

$$SA = 4\pi r^2$$
$$V = \frac{4}{3}\pi r^3$$

What is the right value of pi for a cube so that these two formulas hold for it? Is it the same as the pi-value for a square?

What is the right value of pi for any polyhedron that circumscribes a sphere of radius r?

Is there a good general three-dimensional definition of pi?

What about higher dimensions?

© 2012 James Tanton

APPENDIX: WHEN IS PI THE SAME FOR ALL CIRCLES?

Here is the key question from the first section of this pamphlet:

> Is it all obvious that the value of π is the same for all circles?
>
> Here's a small circle and a large one.
>
>
>
> Is it true that the ratio of the circumference to diameter is the same for each, even to the millionth decimal place?

Here is a quick crude answer:

CRUDE ANSWER: YES!

Recall that if we take a picture to a photocopier and set the machine to a scale factor of 200%, then all lengths in the picture double:

In particular, all lengths for the picture of a circle double, namely, its circumference and its diameter:

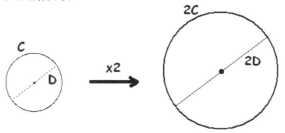

Notice that the ratio of "circumference to diameter" remains the same for each circle:

$$\frac{2C}{2D} = \frac{C}{D}$$

Moreover ... Any circle can be thought of as a scaled version of any other circle (say, with scale factor k). This means that the value of π is the same for each:

$$\pi = \frac{kC}{kD} = \frac{C}{D}.$$

DONE!

This argument is intuitive – it still relies on a belief about how shapes and lengths scale in geometry. Many people find this explanation sufficient, and if this is fine for you, we can leave it there. (But the Nevada circle is still troubling.)

For those that really want to dig deeper, we need to go to the underlying principles of geometry, in particular, the SAS postulate for similar triangles.

THE SAS POSTULATE AND THE VALUE OF PI

The fact that π has the same value for all circles is a logical consequence of the SAS principle in flat geometry. To see why, imagine we have two circles, one of radius r and the other of radius kr for some number k.

Approximate each circle as a union of 12 congruent triangles.

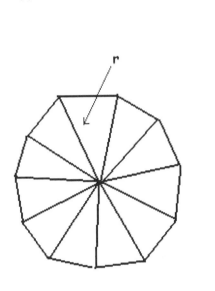
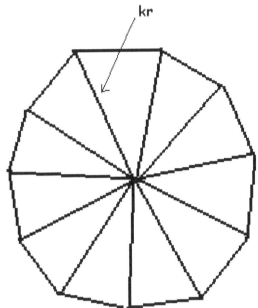

Each of the 24 triangles is an isosceles triangle with angle $30°$ at its apex. (Do you see why?)

Each triangle in the small figure is similar to each triangle in the large figure. This follows from the SAS principle: they have sides about the same angle of $30°$ in the same ratio k.

Because the triangles are similar, the bases of the triangle come in the same ratio k as well. Thus each side length of the large polygon is k times as large as each side length of the small polygon. Consequently, the large polygon has perimeter k times as long as the perimeter of the small polygon.

The value of pi for the small polygon is $\frac{perimeter}{2r}$ and the value of pi for the larger one is $\frac{k \times perimeter}{2rk} = \frac{perimeter}{2r}$. These are the same.

If instead of using 12 triangles, we approximated the two circles using 100 triangles each, the same argument would show that the ratio "perimeter to diameter" again be the same for each figure.

And the same would be true if we used 1000 triangles, or 10000000000 triangles.

Now comes another "leap of faith" …

The ratios of "perimeter to diameter" for each polygonal figure agree every time, and the more triangles we use, the closer each shape comes to being a true circle.

In the limit of using more and more triangles, it might seem reasonable to conclude that the ratio of "perimeter to diameter" for the two original circles would still be the same for each.

Again, this is a belief! (And you might decide you disagree.)

It seems that for circles, we cannot escape some kind of leap of faith. The trouble might be that we humans can only comfortably work with and see straight edges and polygons. Anything that is curved seems to land in the realm of an ideal, just a little bit out of reach.

In any case, this type of argument shows:

> **If you choose to work in a geometry where the standard properties of similar triangles hold, then, with a leap of faith, you must conclude that the value of pi is the same for all circles in that geometry.**

Perhaps surprisingly, there are geometries where the standard properties of similar triangles <u>do not</u> hold, and consequently the value of pi changes for different sized circles!

15. EXERCISE: THE GEOMETRY OF THE EARTH

When we draw (small) circles on the ground and measure the circumferences and diameters, the ratio $\frac{C}{D}$ appears to have the constant value 3.141592…

Suppose we draw a large circle, say one the size of a football field, and draw in its diameter. Do you think the ratio $\frac{C}{D}$ would still be 3.141592… ? Notice that we like to draw both the circle itself *and* the diameter <u>on the ground</u>.

Suppose we draw a circle, and its diameter, that is the size of Nevada. Would the ratio $\frac{C}{D}$ still be 3.141592…? Remember, when living on the Earth, we feel it is appropriate to draw all lines <u>on the surface of the Earth</u>.

Let's go to the extreme: Suppose we draw a circle with center the North Pole and radius one quarter the circumference of the Earth. This circle would be the equator of the Earth.

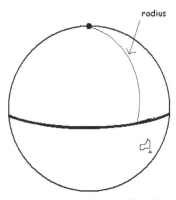

Explain why, for us living on the surface of the Earth, we would have to conclude that the ratio $\frac{C}{D}$ for this circle is 2 and not 3.141592…

THE VALUE OF π IS NOT THE SAME FOR ALL CIRCLES DRAWN ON THE SURFACE OF THE EARTH.

Comment: The value of π for a circle the size of a football field is very close to, but slightly under. 3.141592…. If we were to draw and measure π for a circle the size of Nevada, its value would be perceptibly smaller than 3.141592… .

Weird Ways to Work with Pi

ANSWERS

Page 9: Exercise 1:

a) The diagonal of a square of side-length x is $\sqrt{2}x$ units long and so:

$$\pi_{long} = \frac{4x}{\sqrt{2}x} = \frac{4}{\sqrt{2}} = 2\sqrt{2} \approx 2.828$$

b) The altitude of an equilateral triangle of side-length x is, according to Pythagoras's theorem, $\sqrt{x^2 - \left(\frac{x}{2}\right)^2} = \frac{\sqrt{3}x}{2}$.

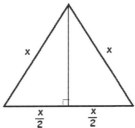

We have:

$$\pi_{triangle} = \frac{3x}{\frac{\sqrt{3}x}{2}} = 2\sqrt{3} \approx 3.464$$

As we shall see on pages 19 and 20 this is not the right value of pi to work with for a triangle! There is a better "diameter" to use.

c) Following the diagram below, the short diameter is $2r = 2 \times \frac{\sqrt{3}x}{2} = \sqrt{3}x$ and so

$$\pi_{hexagon} = \frac{6x}{\sqrt{3}x} = 2\sqrt{3} \approx 3.464$$

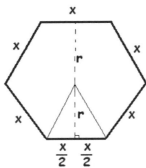

d) Let's compute the diameter of a regular polygon with N sides each of length x. The answer depends on whether N is even or odd.

Even Number of Sides

diameter = 2a

Odd Number of Sides

diameter = a+b

Each diagram has N triangles with angles 2θ at each apex. We have $2\theta = \dfrac{360}{N}$ and so $\theta = \dfrac{180}{N}$ degrees.

Now $\tan(\theta) = \dfrac{x}{2a}$ giving $a = \dfrac{x}{2\tan\theta}$, and $\sin(\theta) = \dfrac{x}{2b}$ yielding $b = \dfrac{x}{2\sin(\theta)}$.

Also, the perimeter of the polygon is Nx.
Consequently:

$$\pi_{N-gon} = \dfrac{Nx}{2 \times \dfrac{x}{2\tan(\theta)}} = N\tan\left(\dfrac{180}{N}\right) \text{ if } N \text{ is even}$$

$$\pi_{N-gon} = \dfrac{Nx}{\dfrac{x}{2\tan(\theta)} + \dfrac{x}{2\sin(\theta)}} = \dfrac{2N}{\dfrac{1}{\tan\left(\dfrac{180}{N}\right)} + \dfrac{1}{\sin\left(\dfrac{180}{N}\right)}} \text{ if } N \text{ is odd.}$$

(Heavens!)

© 2012 James Tanton

For $N = 3$, the equilateral triangle, we have

$$\pi_{triangle} = \frac{6}{\frac{1}{\tan(60)} + \frac{1}{\sin(60)}} = \frac{6}{\frac{1}{\sqrt{3}} + \frac{2}{\sqrt{3}}} = 2\sqrt{3}$$

which agrees with our answer in part b)

For $N = 4$, the square, we have: $\pi_{square} = 4\tan(45) = 4$, as hoped.

For $N = 5$, the regular pentagon, we have:

$$\pi_{pentagon} = \frac{10}{\frac{1}{\tan(36)} + \frac{1}{\sin(36)}} \approx 3.249$$

For $N = 6$,

$$\pi_{hexagon} = 6\tan(30) = 2\sqrt{3} \approx 3.364$$

Continuing this way ...

N	pi-Value
7	3.195
8	3.314
9	3.174
10	3.249
20	3.168
100	3.143
10000	3.141592

It seems that these values are approaching the value of pi for a circle! (Is that surprising?)

Page 13: Exercises 2 and 3:

Let's answer these in terribly clunky ways. As we shall see on page 21 there is a much better approach to this exercise once we fully understand pi.

Suppose the inner figure has side-length x and the gap between the two figures has value h.

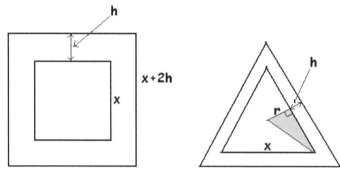

For a square we have $4(x+2h) = 4x + 10$ giving $8h = 10$ and so $h = \dfrac{5}{4}$. Not too bad.

The triangle is trickier. Look at the apothem r. It is part of a 30-60-90 triangle,

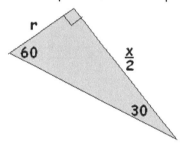

From geometry days, this means that $\dfrac{x}{2} = \sqrt{3}r$ and so $x = 2\sqrt{3}r$. This is a formula for the side-length x of an equilateral triangle in terms of its apothem.

But look at the large triangle, It has apothem $r+h$ and so has side-length $2\sqrt{3}(r+h)$.

Now the perimeter of the large triangle is 10 feet long than that of the inner triangle. So:

$$3 \times 2\sqrt{3}(r+h) = 3 \times 2\sqrt{3}r + 10$$

This gives $h = \dfrac{5}{3\sqrt{3}}$.

(That was hard!)

© 2012 James Tanton

Page 14: Exercise 4:

We need $2\pi r = 170$ so $r = \dfrac{170}{2\pi} \approx 27.1$ cm.

If you actually construct such a wheel it seems surprisingly small!

Page 15: Exercise 5:

Call the diameter of the circle D. Then radius of the circle is $\dfrac{D}{2}$ and the side-length of the square is $\dfrac{8}{9}D$ (one ninth less than the full diameter: trick wording!).

The Egyptians claimed that the areas of these two shapes are approximately the same.

$$\pi\left(\dfrac{D}{2}\right)^2 \approx \left(\dfrac{8}{9}D\right)^2$$

$$\dfrac{\pi}{4}D^2 \approx \dfrac{64}{81}D^2$$

$$\dfrac{\pi}{4} \approx \dfrac{64}{81}$$

$$\pi \approx \dfrac{256}{81} \approx 3.160$$

This is pretty good (but not as good as $22/7 \approx 3.143$).

Page 19: Exercise 6:

If $\pi = 4$ then $2\pi r = 8r$ is indeed the circumference of the square, and $\pi r^2 = 4r^2 = (2r)^2$ is indeed its area.

© 2012 James Tanton

Page 20: Exercise 7:

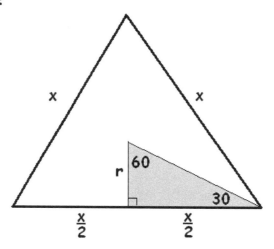

The apothem r of an equilateral triangle of side-length x, we have seen, satisfies $\sqrt{3}r = \dfrac{x}{2}$ and so $r = \dfrac{x}{2\sqrt{3}}$. Thus:

$$\pi_{traingle} = \frac{3x}{2r} = \frac{3x}{x/\sqrt{3}} = 3\sqrt{3}.$$

Now ... The perimeter of the triangle is $3x$ and the area of the triangle is six times the area of the shaded triangle:

$$A = 6 \times \frac{1}{2} \cdot \frac{x}{2} \cdot r = 3 \cdot \frac{x}{2} \cdot \frac{x}{2\sqrt{3}} = \frac{\sqrt{3}}{4}x^2.$$

Do these match $2\pi r$ and πr^2 for $\pi = 3\sqrt{3}$?

Let's see:

$$2\pi r = 2 \times 3\sqrt{3} \times \frac{x}{2\sqrt{3}} = 3x$$

Yes! This is indeed the circumference (perimeter) of the triangle.

$$\pi r^2 = 3\sqrt{3}\left(\frac{x}{2\sqrt{3}}\right)^2 = \frac{\sqrt{3}}{4}x^2$$

Yes! This is indeed the area of an equilateral triangle.

© 2012 James Tanton

Page 20: Exercise 8:

We have already done this work. For the figures on page 44 we have decided that the "diameter" we need to use for both the even- and odd-sided cases is $2a$, And we saw there that $a = \dfrac{x}{2\tan\left(\dfrac{180}{N}\right)}$ in both cases. Thus:

$$\pi_{N-gon} = \frac{Nx}{2a} = \frac{Nx}{x/\tan\left(\dfrac{180}{N}\right)} = N\tan\left(\frac{180}{N}\right)$$ for both even and odd now.

We know that the perimeter of the polygon is Nx. The area of the polygon is N times the area of the triangle shown on page 44 with apex angle 2θ.

$$A = N \times \frac{1}{2}xa = \frac{Nx}{2} \times \frac{x}{2\tan\left(\dfrac{180}{N}\right)} = \frac{N}{4\tan\left(\dfrac{180}{N}\right)}x^2$$

Do the formulas $2\pi r$ and πr^2 give these values? Let's see. (Watch out! Our apothem "r" is being called a on this page.)

$$2\pi a = 2 \times N\tan\left(\frac{180}{N}\right) \times \frac{x}{2\tan\left(\dfrac{180}{N}\right)} = Nx. \quad \text{Good!}$$

$$\pi a^2 = N\tan\left(\frac{180}{N}\right) \times \left(\frac{x}{2\tan\left(\dfrac{180}{N}\right)}\right)^2 = \frac{N}{4\tan\left(\dfrac{180}{N}\right)}x^2. \quad \text{Perfect!}$$

As I said on page 20, we haven't yet hit upon the very best way to think of matters. This work was hard!

Page 21: Exercise 9:
The fact that "$C = 2\pi r$" works for all regular polygons makes this problem easy to solve.

If the inner polygon has apothem r, then its perimeter is $2\pi_{polygon} r$.
If the gap between the polygons is h, then the outer polygon has apothem $r+h$ and perimeter $2\pi_{polygon}(r+h)$. (Draw a picture.)

We are told:

$$2\pi_{polygon}(r+h) = 2\pi_{polygon} r + 10$$

Solving gives:

$$h = \frac{5}{\pi_{polygon}}$$

Page 28: Exercise 10:
This is indeed a mighty tough challenge. I personally do not know a simple way to solve it without using advanced techniques of calculus (Lagrange multipliers). Might you have come up with an elegant approach?

By the way ... All the claims made at the bottom of page 28 turn out to be true.

Page 31: Exercise 11:
a) Just copy the answer to exercise 9 at the top of this page, almost word-for-word!

b) The comment at the bottom of page 27 still applies!

© 2012 James Tanton

Page 32: Exercise 12:

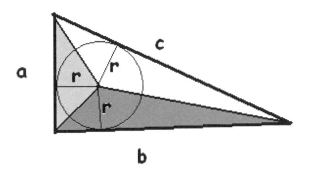

a) The right triangle has area $\frac{1}{2}ab$. The area can also be computed as $\frac{1}{2}ar + \frac{1}{2}br + \frac{1}{2}cr$. Thus $\frac{1}{2}ab = \frac{1}{2}(a+b+c)r$. This gives:

$$r = \frac{ab}{a+b+c}$$

b) Multiply the numerator and denominator each by $a+b-c$:

$$r = \frac{ab(a+b-c)}{(a+b+c)(a+b-c)}$$
$$= \frac{ab(a+b-c)}{(a+b)^2 - c^2}$$
$$= \frac{ab(a+b-c)}{a^2 + b^2 - c^2 + 2ab}$$
$$= \frac{ab(a+b-c)}{2ab} = \frac{1}{2}(a+b-c)$$

c) $\pi_{\text{right triangle}} = \frac{\text{perimeter}}{2r} = \frac{a+b+c}{a+b-c}$

COMMENT: If a,b,c are integers satisfying $a^2 + b^2 = c^2$ it cannot be the case that all three integers are odd. (Then c^2 would be odd, but $a^2 + b^2$, being a sum of two odds, would be even.) Similar reasoning shows that it is impossible for exactly one of the numbers a,b,c to be odd. Thus ... either all three numbers are even, or one of the numbers is even and the remaining two are odd. Either way, $a+b-c$ is sure to be divisible by two.

© 2012 James Tanton

Page 34: Exercise 13:

a) A has units of length square and C has units of length. Thus $\frac{A}{C}$ has units of length, as does $2A/C$.

b) C has units of length and so C^2 has units of length squared. So too does A and so $\frac{C^2}{A}$ is without units.

Page 35: Exercise 14:

The diagram at the bottom of page 30 shows:

$$A = \frac{1}{2}ar + \frac{1}{2}br + \cdots = \frac{1}{2}(a+b+\cdots)r = \frac{1}{2}Cr$$

and so $\frac{2A}{C}$ does indeed equal r,

Page 41: Exercise 15:

The radius here is one-quarter of the length of the equator, $r = \frac{1}{4}C$, and so:

$$\pi = \frac{C}{2r} = \frac{C}{C/2} = 2$$

for this circle.

© 2012 James Tanton